Copyright © 2011 by

Photographs ꞉

by

MW00917632

l

Limit of liability and disclaimer of warranty: The author has made every effort to share his findings and experience, the result of five decades of research and personal experience, in a clear and informative manner. No representations or warranties of any kind are made with regard to the accuracy, applicability, effectiveness, fitness or completeness of the contents of this book and specifically disclaim any implied warranties of merchantability or fitness for a particular purpose. The advice and methods contained herein may not be suitable for every situation. You should consult a professional where appropriate. The author/publisher accepts no liability of any kind for any losses or damages caused, or alleged to be caused, directly or indirectly, from using the information contained in this book.

Outdoor recreational activities are by their nature potentially hazardous. If you participate in outdoor recreational activities, you must assume responsibility for your health and safety and those of others who may be affected by your activity. If you have a health problem or condition, consult with your physician before undertaking any outdoor activity.

Many thanks to...

I would like to thank my good friend and student Morgan Mason for his encouragement and advice whilst writing this book. We spent a lot of time together putting into practice some of my theories about the game and in particular at the beginning of his golfing experience. I must say that he has proven to be a model pupil and although he has reached another sphere of his life in golf now with a handicap of 2, we still find time to discuss and develop in depth the advantages of Good Golf is Easy.

My thanks also go to Mark Mansfield for his fine photography and his golfing contribution by testing the material in this book with success and to his invaluable advice concerning the pre-publishing phase of the book.

Foreword by Morgan Mason

Morgan Mason (left) with John Norsworthy in the South of France.

I have been blessed in many ways over the years. One of those blessings was an impulse to take a golf lesson having never touched a club or had any interest before.

That day I was blessed again to meet John Norsworthy. Since then he has become a true friend and mentor. Although I didn't take that first lesson until well past the age of 40, I was able, with John's guidance and confidence in me, to go from complete novice to a single digit handicap in less than 3 years. Something I didn't really believe was possible but John did. John is not only a great teacher but also a great gentleman. I believe this book will be a tremendous asset to golfers of all levels. The comparisons between the players of yesterday and today are revealing and show that with all the modern technology available now, not much has really changed in the last 100 years. These eternal truths will benefit the game of all golfers and more importantly will make the game easier and more enjoyable.

Thank you John and bless you for making my life so much more enjoyable!

Contents

Chapter 7.
Make your short game precise and dependable   57

Chapter 8.
Putt effectively by putting naturally   67

Chapter 9.
How to play those trouble shots away   73

Chapter 10.
Managing golf's two ultimate adversaries   77

Chapter 11. Questions and answers   85

Afterword   95

About the Author   96

Chapter 1.
Good Golf is Easy!

How can I have the audacity write a book with the title 'Good Golf is Easy' when so often golf can seem anything but easy?

The answer is quite simple and the title crystallized one evening while reading an old favorite from my collection of vintage golf teaching books called *Swing the Club Head* by the wonderful player and teacher Ernest Jones. In that book I came across the phrase, which went along the lines of:

> *"Good golf is easy and easy golf is enjoyable. It is tragic that so many make of it such labor...".*

Never had words sounded so simple and yet so true to me and it is these words, together with my personal experience from my 50 years of teaching as a PGA pro, that inspired me to write this book.

To help illustrate why I say good golf is easy, try this simple exercise. You do not need a golf club or a ball, however you will need a sheet of paper and a pen or pencil. Go on, trust me, even if you are sitting in your favorite comfy chair and don't feel like getting up, go and find them now.

With pen and paper to hand, perform these three simple tasks:

1. In big, bold letters write the words "**Good Golf is Easy!**" in the middle of the paper.

2. Now crumple the sheet of paper into a ball.

3. Finally choose a target, such as a waste paper bin, and throw the paper ball into it.

Well done! You just performed a sequence of tasks requiring complex physical movements and yet I gave no instructions on *how* to do the tasks nor did I give a description of how to move your arms, your shoulders, your hips or any other part of your body when making the throw. Nevertheless, I am sure the paper ball landed near the bin or even inside it.

It was possible for you to make all the necessary movements to achieve the desired result by quite simply using your instincts, your coordination, your sense of feel, your natural rhythm and a good dose of common sense. All are skills that you have learned and developed since you were a small child and all are now innate and natural to you. You did not need to think about how you did what you did, you simply did it. You acted *instinctively*.

Striking a golf ball with a golf club is in many ways very similar and is no more or less complex than the exercise you just performed. To play good golf, you must learn to call upon and rely on the natural skills that you already have within you.

With some practice you would become a paper ball sharp shooter. And by following the practical advice and simple exercises in this short book you will develop the skills needed to play good golf and to enjoy yourself when playing in no time at all!

What is good golf?

'Good golf' is a level of golf where you are able to play your personal best most of the time. It is where you get the most out of your game *and* enjoy yourself when playing. This is regardless of whether you are a beginner or a very experienced player.

It could mean getting your first handicap if you are a beginning player, or reducing your handicap from 24 to 12, or even becoming a single digit handicap player!

Can golf be easy?

"I play golf in the most simple way I know" ~Sam Snead

You do not need to have a perfect looking swing to play good golf, but what all great players have in common is they make playing golf look easy.

There are many expressions in our language that echo this sentiment such as 'take it easy', 'nice and easy' and 'easy does it'.

Easy is an attitude or state of mind that enables us to tackle even the toughest of challenges and I have found that it applies particularly well to the pursuit of learning and playing golf.

Harry Vardon, 1870 - 1937, six times winner of the Open Championship and once winner of the U.S. Open. Here captured in motion just after impact.

Chapter 2.
Eternal golfing truths for weekend golfers

Why amateur scores are not improving

I have often wondered why the average score of the weekend golfer has barely improved over the past century, especially when considering that in the past few decades golf equipment, golf training and the quality of golf courses have all dramatically improved.

Logically, golf scores should have come tumbling down and today's amateurs should, one would imagine, be playing at least as well as the top players from say a hundred years ago.

Surprisingly statistics paint quite a different picture. While tour player scores have improved, those of the average amateur have remained fairly static for decades. Weekend golfers simply have not benefited from modern equipment and training methods to the same extent as touring professionals.

One explanation I often hear for the small difference in scores is that courses are longer today than in the past. While this is true, the increased performance of modern balls, clubs and clothing together with vastly improved golf course conditions cancels out this argument.

I believe the principal reasons that the average score of weekend amateur golfers has not improved are because a) overly technical teaching has become very popular even though it is better suited to full time professionals and b) there is simply too much information available, much of it extremely complex, which rather than making the learning process easier instead creates 'paralysis by analysis'.

Modern touring professionals are extremely talented athletes who train and play golf many hours a day for most days of the year, frequently with the help of a professional coach. They are able to digest the copious amounts of information only because they have a lot of time and because the coach is present to watch and help them work through the many details. This approach does not however suit every type of professional player.

In today's information age there are now many books, DVDs and online sites containing large volumes of information, facts and figures and mechanical procedures which encourage us to dig deeper, to analyze and to dissect the golf swing.

However, because of the great differences between professional players and weekend golfers, the types of instruction should also be suitably adapted to each category of player.

That is precisely what this book offers: simple yet effective instruction and advice that enables average weekend golfers with limited time to play and practice to play well and to enjoy the game.

From my own vast and varied experience of teaching all levels of golf to many thousands of pupils, I have found the most effective methods are drawn from the great players and teachers of the past century who were not only closer to the roots of the great game of golf itself but also knew the secrets of *timeless golfing truths*.

Past masters lead the way...

Allow me to digress and take you for a short visit down memory lane to give you a brief glimpse into some of the wonderful golf that was played around a century ago when course conditions and rules were tougher, equipment was decidedly low tech and ideas such as 'swing analysis' had never been heard of. Here are just a few fine examples of great golf:

In 1870 at Prestwick in Scotland in a competition that would later become *The Open Championship*, Tom Morris junior played and won it with the outstanding score of 149 for 36 holes. This was his third consecutive win of the championship, scoring 157 and 154 the previous two years, which entitled him to keep the championship belt.

In 1892 at Muirfield, The Open Championship was played over 72 holes for the first time and was won by the amateur Mr. H. H. Hilton with a score of 306, an average score of 76.25 shots per round. That was a remarkable feat especially when considering that Muirfield remains a very challenging test of golf even by today's standards.

In the Open Championship in 1906 again at Muirfield, the famous trio known as 'The Triumvirate' made up of James Braid, J. H. Taylor and Harry Vardon finished 1st, 2nd and 3rd respectively. James Braid's four-round score was 300, J. H. Taylor 304 and Harry Vardon 305.

Despite appalling weather during the 1913 US Open, some of the scores were superb. From the first two rounds they included Wilfred Reid with 75 – 72; Harry Vardon 75 – 72; Edward Ray 79 – 70 and Herbert Strong with 75 – 74. Although the tournament was plagued by continuous rain and high winds, placing the ball on the fairway was not allowed.

In 1926 the Open was played at Royal Lytham St. Anne's and was won by Bobby Jones with a score of 291. By way of contrast, on the same course in 1974 Gary Player won with a score of 282. Forty-eight years separate these two fine victories by two great golfers but there is a difference of only nine shots.

Harry Vardon, negotiating a stymie.

What makes these scores even more noteworthy is that even some of the old rules made scoring more difficult than today. For example on the green you could not lift and clean your ball even if it was covered with mud, and if your opponent's ball blocked your line to the hole (known as a 'stymie') you had to putt around or over it.

Also, you always had to play the ball as it lies: even if fairways were waterlogged after a rainstorm there was no relief from casual water. To make matters worse, bunkers were often full of debris and barely raked. The balls frequently broke apart upon impact and the players wore thick clothing that was more suited to going to church than to playing golf.

As so beautifully expressed in one of the finest books I have ever read on the subject of golf *The Greatest Game Ever Played*, when talking of Harry Vardon, Mark Frost said:

"Harry accomplished all of this alone. No caddie, no agent, no traveling swing coach or sports psychologist, no physical therapist, conditioning guru or chiropractor. He played the game without a formfitting cabretta leather glove, custom designer spikes, moisture wicking shirts, titanium metal woods with tempered shock absorbing shafts, or balls with the latent explosive potential of nitroglycerin. His irons were not part of some tungsten – injected, frequency matched progressive set featuring a muscle – backed sweet spot; each one was as quirky and idiosyncratic as its owner. Harry conquered America with ten hickory shafted home made clubs in a canvas bag and an ungainly aerodynamically challenged ball from the hardened sap of an Indonesian palanquin tree".

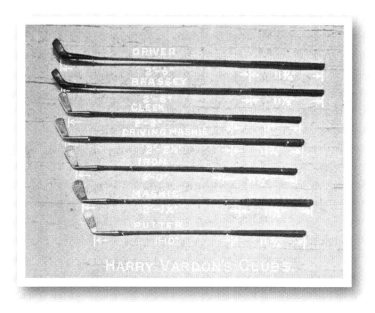

Harry Vardon's hickory shafted, hand-made clubs

Yesteryears' golfers played well because they played simply

In my opinion, the great golfers of yesteryear succeeded in spite of the tougher conditions because they had a simpler approach to learning and playing golf.

Up until 1900 teaching was basically limited to swinging the club back slowly, keeping the eyes on the ball and following through in balance. That was it.

The fine players of one hundred years ago, including Harry Vardon, held the secret to playing good golf without ever realizing it. He and his peers spent very little time analyzing the way in which the club must be moved in order to hit the ball and yet their scores were remarkably good.

They were instead, I believe, more concerned with finding the ball with the club head using their natural instinct and coordination rather than with the mechanics of how to get the club up, down and through.

A common factor I found in my classic golf instruction books was that students were also always taught to rely on their coordination, tempo and natural instinct, with technique occupying a far lesser role than today.

My personal coaching philosophy has been heavily influenced by the great golfers and teachers of the past and what I have observed during my long teaching career – more than fifty years as a PGA teaching professional giving many thousands of lessons to students of all levels – is that the most effective training methods for the modern amateur are in fact very similar the training methods used by the renowned players of yesteryear.

J.H. Taylor (1871–1963) five-time winner of the Open Championship.
Photo circa 1904 showing clothing of the period.

Chapter 3.
Let your hands do the thinking

Most novice golfers use their body excessively when swinging a club in an attempt to make the ball fly further but despite their considerable efforts they rarely meet with success.

Often in golf lessons we are often told how to use our shoulders, hips, legs and just about every other body part but rather surprisingly we rarely hear talk of the important the role of our *hands*. Emphasizing the role of the hands is not a new idea in golf instruction but is in fact as old as the game itself.

Our hands are used for almost every physical activity that we perform. They are extremely sensitive and finely tuned instruments with a large part of the brain devoted to their use. We could say that we literally 'think' with our hands.

It is our capacity to use our hands to work with tools that distinguishes us from all other animal species on the planet and their importance can not be overstated.

To make your golf swing natural, efficient and effortless you must first learn to allow your hands to work freely.

**Left: The hands of James Braid. Here his right hand is opened
so you can see the position of his left thumb on the grip.**

The important role of the hands

Often it is said that the hands should be 'passive', 'inactive' or 'dead'. In my opinion this simply is not true. Instead I believe the hands are very much 'alive' and must be used to feel the swing and the position of the club head.

If you have ever tried to play golf with cold hands you will know just how hard it is to find your rhythm and timing. When the hands are dead they lose all feeling and cause the body to push and heave.

You always swing the club head through to the ball using your arms and hands naturally and without thought just as you do when performing any other everyday task. This is fundamental.

The rest of the body will follow naturally, without thought, exactly as it should to achieve the desired result.

When you learn to capture the *sensation* of swinging the club head with your hands for as long as possible, your body will automatically work in harmony as a whole and you will start to swing smoothly and with ease.

You will learn how to use your hands correctly by following the exercises in the next chapter "Develop your natural ball-striking skills" on page 23.

The dominant hand

Whenever we do something using our hands, we always use one hand more than the other. This is known as the *dominant* or *master* hand. It is the right hand for right-handers and the left for left-handers.

Quite naturally we use our dominant hand for single-handed tasks requiring precision and coordination.

For activities that require both hands, the dominant hand directs while the other assists. For example, when writing a letter I hold the pen in my right hand and steady the paper with my left (yes, you can call me old fashioned if you like). When hammering in a nail, I hold the hammer in my right hand and the nail with my left. When playing pool or billiards, I use my right hand to control the cue and my left hand to steady it.

Regardless of what you may have read or heard elsewhere, in my opinion if you are to achieve your full potential as a golf player you **must** use your dominant hand to feel and control the club while using your other hand just to hold and steady it.

Hands in history

I believe that Ernest Jones and Henry Cotton came the closest to understanding the golf swing and how the weekend golfer can play in the simplest and most logical way possible.

Two other renowned and influential teachers, Leslie King and W.J. Cox, also emphasized the importance of the hands in the swing and are very worthy of a mention.

What follows is a brief summary of what some of the most influential teachers in history had to say about using the hands when playing golf.

Ernest Jones said:

"The club is held in the hands – largely in the fingers – and everything the golfer does with the club is done through them. It is through the hands that he gains the feel of the club. The hands are the medium through which power is transmitted to the club head. 'Touch' is entirely in the hands and the fingers, the fingers impart to the blow the life and vitality which makes the ball travel". ~ Ernest Jones.

He also often said:

"The trouble with the teaching of golf, is that one is taught what a swing produces [body movement], instead of how to produce a swing [club movement]."

His words are music to my ears and are as true today as when he first wrote them. Clubs, balls and clothes may have evolved but the golfer must still swing the club.

Ernest Jones (1887–1965), a World Golf Teachers Hall of Famer and one of the finest golf instructors of all time – this was is spite of losing a leg in WWI.

– Henry Cotton –

"A golfer is only as good as his hands. The hands are the only point of contact with the club and quite understandably they should be in control." ~ Henry Cotton

Sir Henry Cotton was born in 1907 and became a professional golfer at the age of 17. In 1934 he won The Open Championship aged 27 breaking a twelve-year reign by the Americans. In his opening first two rounds he scored 67 and 65! He again won The Open Championship in 1937 and 1948.

He was a Ryder Cup team member in 1929, 1937 and again in 1947 as playing captain. His last appearance was in 1953 as non-playing captain. He was awarded the M.B.E. in 1946.

Sir Henry Cotton (right), 1907 – 1987, three times winner of The Open Championship shown here with John Norsworthy in Spain in 1961.

I have always been influenced by Henry Cotton who I considered to be one of the world's finest teachers and coaches, an opinion shared by many of my fellow professionals who frequently sought his guidance. He had enormous influence on professional golfers of his era and was a brilliant analyst of the golf swing and yet his explanations of it were simple and extremely logical.

I was extremely proud at the time of meeting him to be Head Professional at The Royal Waterloo Golf Club in Belgium, the first club that he had been appointed to as Head Pro many years before.

I visited Mr. Cotton regularly to seek advice. He was never too tired to talk about golf and we discussed golf-teaching methods for hours at a time. It was his unwavering conviction that the right hand gives both strength and touch to the golf shot.

I had seen him hitting 5 iron shots at least 150 yards alternatively with the right hand only and then with the left hand only. At this time he was in his late sixties! He also showed me his famous tire routine, an exercise to build strength and power in the hands (see "Exercise – strengthen your hands and forearms" on page 47).

I had the pleasure of spending one week with him in 1977 in Spain where he taught me many tricks of the trade. The time with him completely confirmed my own theories on the golf swing and his influence continues in my own coaching to this day.

One anecdote that I remember from his hey days, was his devotion to intense practice to the point of having blistered and bleeding hands and on more than one occasion!

One week after his death in 1987 he was awarded the title of Sir Henry Cotton, Knight Commander of the most Honorable Order of St. Michael and St. George.

– Leslie King –

In the foreword to Leslie King's book *Master Key to Good Golf*, Michael Bonallack – several times British Amateur champion and member of the Walker Cup team – wrote:

> *"My only regret in having lessons from Leslie King is that I did not have them sooner".*

I remember in my younger days as an assistant, Mr. King had a huge number of tour professionals working with him and he taught mostly indoors and into a net. In the opening paragraph to his book Mr. King states:

> *"My method of teaching is based upon a free swing of the hands and arms. Just as a player freely swings his arms from his shoulders when walking down the fairway, he must learn to swing his hands and arms with equal freedom and fluency in his golf action".*

This I believe is fundamental to building an easy but effective swing. This is covered more fully in "Chapter 6. Build a solid and powerful swing" on page 41.

Mr. King also said:

> *"The body does not propel the hands and arms at any time. A bad swing is based upon body propulsion, an action in which the hands and arms are set in motion by body movement".*

– W.J. Cox –

I was fortunate enough to have Bill Cox as one of my instructors at the PGA training course in 1961. He was a wonderful teacher and player with a remarkable ability to pass on his message to his pupils in a simple and straightforward way.

In one chapter in his book *Play Better Golf*, he criticizes catch phrases often used in golf. When referring to the phrase 'let the club do the work', this was reply:

> *"What on earth are you there for? There is no 'let' about it. Your hands, at your dictation, control the club throughout the swing and they make the club do the work."*

He also wrote:

> *"One of the simplest ways of distinguishing a good golfer even before he strikes a ball, is to watch how he handles his club. You will notice that the hands immediately assume control and in the 'waggles' which precede the swing."*

> *"There is an obvious display of power as the hands 'whip' the club-head through with speed and precision at the bottom of the swing."*

And he went on to say:

> *"I try to make my pupils see that the hands are the only part of the player in direct contact with the club: therefore they must have complete control and must be trained to bring the club-head to the ball square and at maximum speed".*

Right: The hands of Harry Vardon. Once again the right hand is opened so you can see the position of his left thumb on the grip.

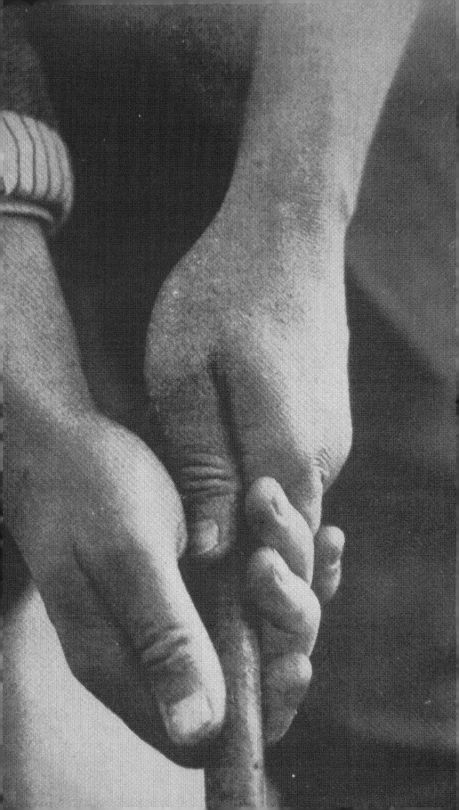

Chapter 4.
Develop your natural
ball-striking skills

With a little practice playing golf will become just as easy and natural as most of your other everyday activities.

The following drills and exercises are extremely important since they build the foundations of your ball striking skills. They do so by soliciting and developing the abilities that you already have while at the same time providing you with immediate feedback for your actions. Repeat these exercises frequently and you will progress both rapidly and simply.

❉ The instructions in this book are written with right-handed players in mind but they work equally well for left-handed players: for left-handed players where you read 'right hand', just read this to mean 'left-hand' and vice-versa. ❉

Get the feel of a solid strike

Striking a golf ball is simple! Always remember this.

The following exercises develop your feel for solid contact with the ball. They take around 30 minutes to perform. For each exercise place the ball on a low tee and use a 7 iron.

1. **Right hand only** (left photo). Play 5 – 10 very short shots of no more than 30 yards using only your right (master) hand. Do this until you feel that the impact with the ball is perfect.

2. **Left hand only** (center photo). Repeat the previous exercise using only your left hand. After a few attempts, you should notice it was much easier when using your right hand.

3. **Both hands.** In this drill, use your left hand to hold the club (but not direct it) and your right hand to provide you with a sense of feel and control. With the club in both hands play 10 short shots of no more than 50 yards.

4. **Now with your feet together** (right photo), play some half-swing shots using your hands and arms to do the work. You will find that quite naturally and with no conscious thinking that striking a golf ball is simple.

5. **Normal stance, half-swing.** With a normal stance, play some half-swing shots. After striking ten or so good shots, move on to the next exercise.

6. **Normal stance, full swing.** Repeat the previous exercise but now make a full swing allowing your body to turn freely and naturally.

In no time at all you will start to feel a wonderful tempo and the impact with the ball will be light and crisp. You will start to understand that with very little effort the ball can actually travel quite far.

At this point, believe it or not, your swing will start to contain all the ingredients of the swings of our great golfing predecessors from one hundred years ago.

✳ *Memorize the feeling of a perfect impact as the club head meets the ball: a nice crisp, clean 'click' or 'tick'. Commit this sensation to memory and call upon it whenever you prepare to play a shot. This is the first and most important step on your road to discovering that Good Golf is Easy.*✳

See, feel, strike

One of the challenges in golf is that we strike a stationary ball from a stationary position, which leaves far too much time to think about *how* to strike it. Often we can get so busy thinking about how to swing that we completely forget the main objective, which simply is to *find the ball with the club head.*

In other sports where the ball is in motion, such as tennis, there is no time to think about how to move or swing, instead our priority is to play the ball.

The following exercises develop coordination between your eyes, hands and club by using your natural instincts and your sense of feel. You will have no time to think about your swing but be prepared to expect some rather amazing results.

For all exercises, place the ball on a low tee and play around ten shots for each of the drills.

1. **Find the ball.** Using a 7 iron, stand to the ball as if playing a normal shot. Now position the club head at least 12 inches *away* from the ball. The club head can really be anywhere you like: inside, outside, in front of, or behind the ball, it is up to you and is not important.

    Starting your swing from this unusual position, swing back and through finding the ball with the club head.

Within a few minutes of playing shots in this way, you will start to strike the ball as well as, if not better than, before. You will be completely unable to think of how to swing the club as finding the ball will be your only priority.

2. **Vary club head position.** Vary the starting position of the club head and repeat the previous exercise.

3. **Use a 5 wood or hybrid.** Repeat the previous two exercises but this time use a 5 wood or a hybrid/rescue club.

4. **Driver.** Finish off by playing some shots this way with your driver.

You will be amazed at how well you strike the ball when you don't think about how to do it. And you can also impress your friends with your newly found ability to play trick shots with ease!

When on the golf course and you are ready to play, recall the feedback and sensations from these exercises (but not how you did the exercises or how you got the results).

✷ Remember; when you swing the club all you need to do is ***find the ball with the club head***. ✷

Find the ball with the club head

Above all else I believe that you must *find the ball with the club head.* And as mentioned earlier, I strongly believe that the right or *master* hand provides you with a sense of touch and feel allowing you to be aware of what is happening with the club head.

These keys were the secrets to success used by the greatest players and teachers in history and they still apply today especially for beginners and high handicap players.

Practice these exercises regularly

Practice the exercises in this chapter on a regular basis all your golfing lifetime regardless of your current level and your rate of progress. They will keep you in touch with your instinctive sense of feel and coordination.

Practice in the practice area, play on the course

As with all the training exercises in this book, remember that the practice area is the only place to practice.

When on the golf course, at no time should you be thinking about *how* to swing the club or about any other technicality. Your thinking will get in the way of your instincts and natural timing, often with disastrous results.

When on the golf course, you must simply play.

Club head magic

To conclude this chapter about using our instincts and natural ability, I would like to share a short anecdote with you about one of the finest trick shot artists in the world Noel Hunt.

I had the great pleasure of working and becoming friends with Noel. He had a show called *Club Head Control* where he would perform some of the most amazing feats with club and ball. These were only possible because of his perfect coordination between his hands, the club head and the ball.

John Norsworthy (left) with Noel Hunt in the South of France.

Harry Vardon
addressing the ball
with a cleek (equivalent
of today's 1 iron).

Chapter 5.
Set up correctly for a reliable swing

In the previous chapter I asked you to try several practical exercises without giving you any explanation of technique. Although this may seem like doing things backwards it is in fact quite intentional as you must first and foremost use and develop your natural skills of coordination.

Your next step is to work on your *setup* or *address* position. Correct setup is vital since most problems during the swing arise even before you start to move.

Your setup must also become part of an identical *pre-shot routine* before you play each shot (more about that at the end of this chapter).

With the correct address your swing will follow almost by itself and your shots will become consistent and your progress rapid.

P. G. A. is normally the abbreviation used to mean *Professional Golfers' Association*. Here we will use P. G. A. as a memo-aid for the three key points of the setup: **P**osture, **G**rip and **A**lignment.

Players from the past opted for a comfortable yet dynamic posture before attempting to swing the club. I recommend you adopt a very similar stance.

The morphology of each player influences his or her address position. For example, the way you place your feet when at address is the same as how you place them when walking. The width of your stance will also be similar to the size of your paces when walking. Taller people, as with the size of their paces, naturally have a wider stance.

Regardless of your height and your physical build, there are some common points you must apply:

1. Incline your body forward at the waist with the upper body straight, the knees slightly bent and the arms hanging straight down from the shoulders.

2. You should have a dynamic feeling similar to a tennis player waiting to receive a service or a soccer goalkeeper facing a penalty. Your weight should be evenly distributed between the balls and heels of your feet.

Ball position

When taking your posture you must correctly position your feet relative to the ball. This position varies slightly with each club you play. Here are the four basic ball positions:

1. Driver or wood from a tee

Position the ball in line with the inside of your left foot. This forward ball position enables you to strike the ball on the upward path of the through swing and launch the ball on an upward path.

When making your practice swing, always swing the club at least an inch or so above the ground – about the same height as when the ball is teed up.

When the ball is truck properly from a tee shot, often the tee remains in the ground. Avoid making divots on the teeing area, your shots will be better and the green keeper will be most appreciative.

2. Fairway woods from the ground (left)

Position the ball between the left heel and centre of the stance. During your practice swing you may brush the grass with your club since the ball is played from the ground.

3. Long/medium irons and rescue/hybrid clubs (right)

Position the ball slightly left of the centre of your stance.

4. Short irons from 8 iron to sand wedge (left)

Position the ball in the middle of your stance for all normal shots and between the middle and your right foot for a lower 'punch' type ball flight.

– *Grip* –

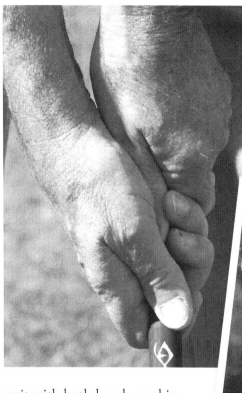

The *grip* is just another way of saying how you hold the club.

The club should be held in such a way that the two hands work as a single

unit with both hands working perfectly in unison. This is key to a good swing.

The most commonly used types of grip are the overlapping/Vardon grip, the interlocking grip and the double-handed/baseball grip (see photos opposite).

Harry Vardon, although not the first to use this style of grip, made the *Vardon* grip popular more than one hundred years ago and today it is by far the most widely used in golf. Either of the two others types of grip are also quite acceptable.

The club is held with both the palm and the fingers. The thumb and forefinger of the right hand are particularly important, as they are the 'trigger fingers' that give control and help to produce the sensation of feeling where the club head is as it swings, which in turn produces much better timing.

  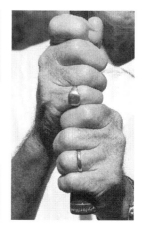

Vardon (overlapping) grip   **Interlocking grip**   **Baseball grip**

Note: *The grip will always be firm but the wrists retain their mobility.*

At this point it would be advisable to have a professional go through the grip with you since depending on your style, strength and swing it must be personalized accordingly.

Remember, in order to progress you must have a good grip. Even if at the beginning any changes that are necessary seem awkward, have patience and you will be rewarded.

– *Alignment* –

For each shot, you must first carefully select your target and then align yourself perfectly for that target.

Start by tracing an imaginary line from your ball to your target – this is your *target line*. Now draw a second imaginary line level with your feet and parallel to the target line. This is your *alignment line* along which you must align your feet, hips and shoulders.

If you extend both lines, the target line goes to your target and your alignment line slightly to the left of your target. To help you visualize this, imagine a narrow railroad track leading from you to your target: one track is your target line and the other is the alignment line.

By ensuring your body correctly aligned, you automatically ensure that your swing is also on plane (more about that in "Swing on plane" on page 48).

Develop your pre-shot routine and stay with it

Develop a pre-shot routine that is identical for each shot. It should always take less than 10 seconds and must include these points:

- Before taking up the address, always stand behind the ball and look in the direction of the hole and try to visualize the eventual flight of the ball

- Come back to the ball and make either a full practice swing or just a warm up half-swing (my preference), the choice is yours.

- Address the ball and make two small waggles, 2 seconds of concentration, breath deeply but quietly, think 'relax' or 'easy' and then fire away.

This is a suggested routine. You can adapt it or invent your own but please remember to keep it to a maximum of ten seconds or you may find that you have fewer and fewer playing partners.

If you choose to make a full practice swing each time, be sure that it is an exact rehearsal of the actual shot to be played. My personal preference is for a small half-swing to become aware of the feel between my hands and the club head.

When addressing the ball, do not *over* concentrate. Doing so will cause you to 'freeze' and the beginning of your swing will likely be more of a snatch than an easy swing. Instead, try to be in motion at all times even if the movements are imperceptible, you will feel the difference and it will allow you to 'pull the trigger' smoothly.

After the shot, good or bad, do not dwell on the result. Especially after a bad one as the risk will be to carry negative thoughts into the next shot. I love the often-quoted reply made by Arnold Palmer when asked by a journalist "*What is the most important shot in golf?*" Mr. Palmer answered "*The next one!*"

Harry Vardon.

Chapter 6.
Build a solid and powerful swing

This chapter will teach you a swing that is reliable, repeatable and easy to perform. You will learn to strike the ball solidly and with authority and your shots will become both long and accurate.

1. Start with the finish

The *finish* is tremendously important in a golf swing having far greater value than being simply the result of what has gone on before it. A good finish influences the swing path that precedes it.

I teach my beginning students to swing to the finish position before teaching the backswing movement. While this may seem illogical, I have found that doing so greatly simplifies the quest to create the correct swing path and to keep the swing on plane (more about that later).

In other sports such as tennis and squash, the finish is taught to the players with the same importance as for the rest of the movement. To harness the full power of your swing in golf, you must learn to stay in balance throughout the swing right through to the finish.

The better your balance at the end of the swing, the greater your freedom of movement during the swing. Your swing will become smoother and you will strike the sweet spot of the club more often.

Exercise – swing through to the finish

Ernest Jones   1.   3.

1. Using a 5 iron, with your feet together and the ball on a low tee, hit 10 shots and hold the finish position for 3 seconds after each shot.

2. Repeat the previous exercise but this time using a 3 wood.

3. Now with your feet in the normal address position, repeat exercises 1 and 2. Again hold the finish position for three seconds after each shot.

4. Using a 5 iron but no ball, start with your club in the finish position. Now swing the club back and then through once again to the finish position. Hold the finish for three seconds. Repeat this several times.

5. This time with a ball, repeat the previous exercise. Even if this exercise is a little difficult at first you should persevere since the resulting improvement in balance and timing is very noticeable.

Use a mirror where possible and always hold the finish for 3 seconds. The next time you play on the course, play every shot including putts with a minimum three-second pause at the end of each stroke.

2. Groove your swing

| 1. | 2. | 3. |

1. Without a club, place your two hands together as in the address position.

2. Leaving your left hand in place, swing your right arm up into a throwing position.

3. Return the right arm to the address position and go to the finish position with the left hand only. Repeat these actions several times.

4. Holding a 7 iron at the head end, repeat the above exercise passing the club from one hand to the other while swinging through.

5. Now hold the club normally with both hands and make some full swings while recalling the positions of your right and left hands from the previous two exercises. If you followed all the previous steps, your swing will already be starting to look good.

6. Finally, play around ten shots from a low tee recalling the same feeling as for the practice swings in steps 1 to 4.

Repeat the previous drills several times. Doing so will program you to remember the sensations of a correct full swing. You should now start to be able to hit some great shots automatically with an easy swing.

To make the exercises even more effective, practice in front of a mirror or record and watch your swing using a video camera. Practice this exercise frequently making it a part of your regular practice sessions and warm up sessions.

3. Swing freely

In my *Good Golf is Easy* demo show, I strike a sequence of sixteen balls one after the other in time to the music from the *Blue Danube*. To strike all of the balls correctly I must concentrate fully on rhythm and tempo, putting aside any thoughts of technique.

After striking three or four balls, I become aware that as I swing there is a force trying to pull the club from my hands – that of centrifugal force. Centrifugal force can only be created by allowing the arms and hands to work freely around the rotation of the body.

A 'swing' is so called because the club swings about the body. The more you allow your arms and hands to move freely about the body, the greater the centrifugal force and the greater the distance the ball will fly when struck. To play good golf easily you must learn to *swing* the club head.

The effects of centrifugal force are often neglected in teaching today but were discussed once again by Ernest Jones in his book *Swing the Club Head.*

Fred Couples, Ernie Els and Sam Snead are excellent examples of players with easy and powerful swings. They do not appear to force their swing and yet one has the impression of great power: this is centrifugal force at work.

Exercise – feel the force

1. Place a ball on a low tee, put your feet together and strike 10 shots with a 5 iron.

2. Repeat the above exercise, this time using a 3 wood.

3. For even greater effect, try the previous two exercises but with your eyes closed. This is great way to *feel* the centrifugal force in your swing.

You will notice that if you try to force a shot by using excessive body power, you will lose not only all sensation of centrifugal force of the club pulling from your hands but also you will lose your balance.

To accentuate the feeling of the club pulling from your hands, try the above exercises while sitting on a barstool or on a chair.

4. Make your swing smooth and powerful

The winners of long driving competitions often are ex-baseball players and baseball players are frequently great golfers too. When you look at their swings, it is not surprising since their swings are powerful and flowing.

As an everyday golfer, you can get more power and smoothness in your swing and give your shots more distance by learning a more baseball-like swing. The following exercise will help you with this:

1. Take a 5 wood and while standing upright, hold the club in front of you and parallel to the ground (photo, left).

2. Keeping the club in this position, make a full back swing parallel to the ground (photo, center). The hands and arms are automatically in the correct position with the body reacting naturally.

3. Now make the through-swing to the same position in exactly the same way (photo, right). You will find the movement easy and completely natural.

Exercise – strengthen your hands and forearms

Warning! Do not try this exercise if you suffer from tendonitis, golf elbow, or have any similar type of strain or injury. Consult your physician before attempting this exercise to see whether a soft impact bag may be used instead.

For this exercise you will need a car tire (an old worn tire is perfect but any will do). Choose a low lofted club such as a 2 or 3 iron and take your address position with the face of the club placed against the right center of the tire.

1. With your right hand only and gripping slightly down on the club, make five half-swings striking the center of the tire while ensuring the clubface is square (not the toe or the heel of the clubface but the center) at impact.

2. Still holding the club with your right hand, make five back-handed swings contacting the back of the club on the left exterior side of the tire.

3. Repeat the previous two exercises using your left hand only.

4. Now grip the club normally with both hands and make five half-swings against the tire.

5. Repeat the previous exercise but this time make five backhanded swings contacting the back of the club against the left exterior side of the tire.

6. Finally, step away clear of the tire, turn the club upside down and hold the shaft just below the head with the right hand only. Now swing the club back and forth freely (no contact with the tire) for around thirty seconds. This will free up the muscles you have just worked on.

7. Repeat the previous step with the left hand only.

Repeat this exercise regularly to build more strength in your wrists and arms *and* improve your ball striking. The impact with the tire immediately shows if the clubface is square at impact or not.

A more comfortable, although less effective, alternative to the tire is the 'impact bag', which is a heavy-duty version of a beanbag.

5. Swing on plane

E. Blackwell

The final building block to good ball striking is learning to swing 'on plane'. The swing plane describes the angle of the club shaft (viewed down the target line) during the swing.

Correct address and an on plane swing ensure the club head follows a slightly inside-to-outside or inside-to-straight path relative to the target line as it nears impact. This club head path is essential for making your shots long and accurate.

Exercise – find the center ball

This exercise helps to develop a swing that is easy to keep on plane. Use a 7 iron.

1. Place three balls on the ground as shown in the photos. Place the center ball on a low tee.

2. Set up to the center ball with a fairly closed stance (right foot further away from the target line than the left).

3. Now play some half-swing shots, striking the center ball while avoiding the two outer balls. You will automatically find the correct swing path without thinking about it. When it is incorrect, you will strike either the inner or the outer ball.

4. As you warm up and your confidence grows, start making some full swings.

5. Now play the center ball from the ground.

6. Finally, repeat the exercise using a 5 wood from a low tee.

Work on this exercise for each of your next several practice sessions and the correct swing path will start to happen naturally.

Exercise – swing plane visual checks points

This exercise provides you with some visual checkpoints to further ensure your swing is on plane.

1. Place two clubs on the ground level with your toes and parallel to the target line (photo above).

2. Bring the club shaft back so it is parallel to the ground. At this checkpoint, the shaft should also be aligned with the clubs on the ground, which are parallel with your target line (photo right).

3. Continue back with the club to make a half to three-quarter

backswing and then start the through-swing. When the shaft is once again parallel to the ground, check that the shaft is parallel to the club shafts on the ground.

4. Continue with the movement bringing the club head to the ball impact position (photo left).

5. Practice these partial swings using the checkpoints several times.

Practice this exercise regularly and your swing will almost always be on plane.

When playing a shot, simply swing in balance through to the finish and the club head will automatically follow the correct swing path (swing plane) with very little error. It may also be helpful to visualize throwing the club head to the target, as if throwing a ball.

Full swing summary

We can say that there are four simple phases to a full swing: 1) address the ball, 2) swing back, 3) swing though and 4) finish.

Many of the following details will happen naturally by themselves and you need not think about them when playing. Your priority when playing, as before, is to find the ball with the club head.

Remember that the swing is single continuous movement and should always be viewed as such.

1. Address the ball

Address the ball using your pre-shot routine.

To get the feel of the club head, waggle the club two or three times. This is a small backward and forward movement of the club head just behind the ball using the wrists and arms only. This keeps you dynamic and ready for the movement to come. Our golfing ancestors always used this preliminary with excellent results.

2. Swing back

Your legs remain quiet during the back swing and the through-swing to provide you with a solid base from which to throw.

To start the back swing, move the arms and hands on a natural inside path like the opening of a door. Allow the body to follow this rotation and keeping the left arm firm but not stiff, place the club at the top of the swing using the right arm as in a throwing motion, (see "Groove your swing" on page 43).

The weight at this time will be mostly on the right leg. The body will react to the hands and arms and not the contrary.

3. Swing through

The *through-swing* is getting the club from the top to the finish while finding the ball with the club head. I intentionally use the term *through-swing* to replace the combined terms down-swing and impact.

Almost all my beginning students over my years of teaching have a tendency to decelerate the club before impact resulting in all sorts of shot errors and in particular a loss of distance.

This deceleration is largely due to thinking too much about the mechanics of the downswing, which results in a hit *at* the ball and a virtual stopping of the swing movement.

By getting your back swing correct and conducting the through-swing as a single, smooth movement, you will accelerate naturally through the impact area. Remember that the ball is not the terminus of the swing, the finish is.

From the top of the back swing you are now in a position ready to throw. The through-swing is then really quite a natural sequence of events.

Your weight transfers to your left leg, bringing your hands and arms into action, the same way as when throwing a ball. Resistance is felt on the left side of your body as it prepares to receive the attack of the right arm and hand coming through. This will cause a powerful strike of the ball, sending it straight and far.

4. Finish

To successfully complete your through-swing, you always must decide to finish the movement completely. This unfortunately is not automatic because of our desire to hit at the ball.

For every shot you must be in perfect balance at the end of your swing. If you are in balance at the end, you have made a swing, otherwise you have made a hit. Remember to *find the ball with the club head* and not hit at it.

Facing page: Joyce Wethered (Lady Heathcoat-Amory) 1901–1997, widely regarded as the greatest British female player of all time. Here showing great balance, poise and power.

Henry Cotton

Chapter 7.
Make your short game
precise and dependable

The short game is a vital element to playing good golf and as with putting, when you get good in this area your scores will greatly improve even if your full swing shots are not yet perfect.

The short game covers shots from the green-side to around sixty-five yards away. It includes chips, pitches, lob shots and bunker shots.

Bullet-proof chipping

Chipping is one of the most important shots in the game especially for the high handicap player. Chipping is played in almost the same way as your putting.

You can chip using any club in the bag but often a 6 or 7 iron is preferred to give the shot a low trajectory that runs for at least three quarters of its distance along the ground.

You can chip up to 25 yards from the green provided that the rolling portion of the shot is on short grass or on the green itself.

The easiest and most reliable technique I recommend for chipping is as follows:

1. Take your address position and grip as for putting.

2. Lift the heel of the club off the ground putting the shaft in a more vertical position. This makes the shot easier to play and gives more consistent results. It also helps the club pass through longer grass than when using the whole face of the club.

3. Place the ball in the middle of your stance.

4. Make some practice swings, **ensuring there is no contact with the ground**. This shot requires that impact with the ball to be very clean and even a topped ball will work just fine.

5. Now using the same swing as your practice swing, strike the ball cleanly.

You will be amazed at the precision of the shot and how easy it is to ensure consistently good direction. This shot alone will help you reduce your number of putts per round, as you will rarely be far from the hole.

The chip can be played anywhere around the green such as uneven or bare lies and even from the edges of bunkers.

When there is less green to play with and you need more airtime with less roll, use the same technique as before but using a more lofted club such as a 9 iron or a pitching wedge.

You may at times see professionals using a fairway wood from just

off the green and I suggest that you also learn and practice the previous technique with this club too.

Because the sole of the club is large, you almost eliminate the risk of hitting a fat shot. It is also very effective for chipping when the ball has nestled down into the grass.

Using a 5 wood or hybrid club and with a stance similar to putting, grip down to a natural position on the club and use the same putting motion as before.

Experiment with this shot from various situations just off the green. I am sure that after trying it out a few times that you will soon add it to your repertoire of most useful shots.

Simple and reliable pitching

Play the pitch shot when you want to pitch the ball over an obstacle, such as a bunker, a mound or an area of rough, where you need more air time and less roll. The ideal club for this shot is the pitching wedge or sand wedge.

The technique is really quite simple:

1. Take an open stance to the target (left foot further away from the target line than the right).

2. For a medium trajectory shots, center the ball in your stance. For lower shots, position the ball towards the inside of your

right foot and for higher shots towards the inside of your left foot.

3. Cock the wrists just a little earlier on the back swing than for a regular shot but not excessively so.

4. Make the swing using mostly your arms and hands and letting the body follow.

5. Keep the legs and body as quiet as possible.

6. Use a back swing that is a little shorter than the through swing. This helps to accelerate through impact.

Important! Progressively transfer your weight to your left side during the downswing so that at impact there is more weight on your left leg than your right. If you find that you hit the ground before the ball, remember to transfer your weight earlier to the left side.

Exercises – pitching

1. To ensure that your pitching practice is successful, start by hitting several shots with a pitching wedge or sand wedge from a low tee until impact with the ball is good.

2. Alternate between playing one ball from the tee then one ball from the ground. Eventually play shots only from the ground. Start by practicing ground shots only from good lies.

3. Using the same length swing for the following shots, play ten balls from inside your right foot then ten from the inside your left foot.

You will notice that the different ball position is all that is required to create low and high ball flights.

By keeping to this simple approach, you will discover that the loft of the club does all the work of producing the correct ball flight.

High, floating lob shots

A lob shot is a very high, floating shot where the ball doesn't travel very far. It is very easy to play if you keep to the following basic guidelines and use a 58° or 60° lob wedge.

- Follow the same technique used for pitch shots. The extra club loft will do the work giving you all the height you need

- Never try to play a lob shot too far – it is intended for creating precise, short distance, high flying, soft landing shots

- For extra finesse try a longer, slower swing with a big follow through. You will be delighted with the result

- A word of warning, do not play using this technique from bare lies. The correct technique is explained on page 73.

Bunker Shots

After putting, the bunker shot is the easiest shot in golf because for the first time you do not have to actually hit the ball. What a relief!

The majority of bunker shots are made using a 56° sand wedge although a 60° lob wedge can be very useful for deep, steep walled bunkers close to the green and where there is very little green to work with.

Your wedges do not necessarily have to match your irons and I strongly recommend that you use steel shafted wedges for sand shots.

Technique – bunker shot

The lines drawn in the sand in the photo are for your guidance only.

1. Take a similar address as for pitching and putting, using a fairly wide, open stance (left foot further back, feet aligned left of your target).

2. Snuggle your feet nicely into the sand with the ball in the middle of your stance. Aim the clubface to your target.

3. Swing the club working the arms and the hands freely from the body.

4. Cock the wrists earlier during the back swing than for regular shots. This will create a more upright plane.

5. Fix your eyes on a spot of sand 2 inches to the right of the ball. Make sure you hit this area of sand before the ball. Swing the club head on a path parallel to your toes. This will automatically 'cut' the clubface across the ball and trap sand between the clubface and the ball. Because you are striking sand first rather than the ball, you can make a big swing with conviction and the ball will come out softly.

Note. Three secrets to great bunker play, especially for the higher handicapper, are:

1. Keep the clubface square to the target.

2. Accelerate through impact and follow through.

3. Practice sand shots without a ball, sending only sand onto the green. This simple technique is great for achieving the right feeling of impacting the sand.

Finally, do not be greedy with sand shots. Just remember the old saying '*in for one, out for one*'.

J.F. Laidlay

Chapter 8.
Putt effectively by putting naturally

As mentioned in the previous chapters, learning to play golf is easier when you rely more on your natural instinct than when following complicated recipes. The same is true for putting.

Our golfing forefathers putted naturally and simply and it is why they scored so well. Looking at photos from the wonderful book by George W. Bedlam published in 1904, I observe three common factors:

1. Their stance is open and wide.

2. Their left elbow is away from their body and pointing slightly towards the hole.

3. Their eyes are always directly over the ball.

If any of my students experience difficulties when putting, I get them to try this position. The results are simply spectacular. Invariably they start to putt better, their confidence increases dramatically and any fear of putting virtually disappears.

Gaining confidence is a major step to finding success on the greens.

When watching a child or someone who has never played golf before who tries putting for the first time, they invariably adopt a position similar to the one described above. It is quite natural for them to face in the direction of the target as much as they can.

Facing the target is also the natural position when playing darts, bowling or making a throw. A wide stance creates a feeling of great stability and the elbow slightly towards the hole improves aiming along the putting line.

This putting stance inevitably means using the wrists and hands more than in a conventional stance. However, as with my approach to teaching the full swing, this more natural and instinctive approach has yielded excellent results in virtually all my students.

Completely excluding wrist action, as often recommended in modern day teaching, is so unnatural that it creates stiffness, tension and loss of feel. The result is an enormous difficulty to judge distance.

Dave Pelz, a prolific writer and expert on the short game, states that 80% of bad putting is a result of poor judgment of length and not of direction.

Exercise – hole increasingly long putts

Practice the following exercises using a really comfortable position based on the previous recommendations and photos.

1. Start by putting 2 feet from the hole. Each time you hole out, move the ball an additional 2 feet from the hole and putt again. If you miss a putt, stay at the same distance until you hole out.

2. Now, repeat the previous exercise and this time see how far you can get in 15 minutes. This is one of the simplest but most effective putting improvement exercises that I know.

3. Finally, repeat the previous exercise but this time look at the hole while you putt. This will seem odd at first, but quickly it becomes quite natural. Just think of other sports such as darts where you look at the target while making your throw.

Exercise – center your putts for consistent length

During my early years as an assistant at the Roehampton Golf Club near London, my former employer and coach George Gadd (who incidentally was one of Britain's best putters when in his prime) held the opinion that to putt well, you must strike the ball perfectly.

I totally agree with his point of view. The following exercise will help you learn to strike the ball perfectly when putting.

Start around 7 yards from the hole and use the same strength of putt for each of the following exercises:

1. Putt 3 balls striking the ball on the toe of the putter.

2. Putt 3 balls striking the ball on the heel of the putter.

3. Putt 3 balls striking the ball in the middle of the putter.

If you used the same force for each putt, only balls hit using the middle of the putter face reach the hole while the others will be short. Many bad putts are usually because of poor ball striking rather than because of bad judgment – this exercise will prove this.

Exercise – grooving center strikes on the putter face

To further improve centering the ball with your putter, try the following exercise: tape 2 matchsticks vertically to the face of the putter, a little wider apart than the ball and equidistant from the vertical centerline of the putter face.

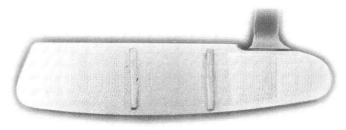

Now repeat the exercise "hole increasingly long putts". You will find that only centered putts work. This is a great way to consistently center your ball strikes when putting.

When putting just remember to take an easy putting stance and concentrate on the quality of your ball striking, rather than focusing on technique. Your putting will soon be as good as the old and modern masters.

Great green reading

While putting is essential to good golf, learning to read greens is fundamental to putting successfully.

Here are the most important points to remember:

- When walking towards the green, take a look at the general topography: where is the high point and where is the low point? This will give you the general idea of the slope that you can expect and the direction that your ball is likely to take.

- When studying the line of your putt, just imagine water coming from the hole and seeing which direction it will flow. Again, this is another good indicator.

- If you see no slope at all, do not invent one. Just putt straight and concentrate on getting the distance right.

- Study the grass itself: has the green been cut recently? Is the green humid or dry?

- Watch and learn from your partner's putts and how the ball behaves on the green. By being observant, you will gain a lot of valuable information in a very short time, further enabling you to make the right decision before you putt.

- Grass grows at an amazingly fast pace! Beware of the difference in the speed the greens between the earlier and later greens, especially if the round is played over a five-hour period (which unfortunately can often be the case these days). There will be a significant difference between the first holes and the last few holes.

- If you start your game early in the morning, the morning dew will burn off as the day warms and if your game finishes in the evening, humidity may start to settle on the greens as the day draws to a close. The humidity plays and important role in green speed and how much a putt will break. This gives even more reason to take just a little more time when reading the greens.

- As a final note, you will not wish to be accused of slow play, so always do your green reading whilst waiting for your turn to putt!

Mother knows best...

I would like to close the putting chapter with a short anecdote.

My mother proved to me that putting was the easiest part of golf. She had never played golf in her life, but whilst waiting for my father to finish his round she alternated between knitting and putting.

After several months of this diet, she became a very good putter indeed and I cannot remember one time that either my father or myself was able to beat her on our club's putting green!

Harry Vardon negotiating a stymie. Fortunately this is one shot you no longer have to tackle

Chapter 9.
How to play those trouble shots away

There are all sorts of 'trouble shots' that you will encounter. Here are the three most common and how to deal with them.

1. Playing from bare lies (tight lies)

A bare or tight lie means that the ball is lying on a hard, smooth surface with little or no grass. This usually scares the life out of the average golfer and invariably they either top the ball or hit the ground heavily before the ball.

The secret here is to make contact with the ball first. To do this, place the ball nearer your right foot and your hands forward of the ball.

Make a partial swing and start to transfer your weight to your left side before impact. You should have the impression of hitting down onto the back of the ball, which will happen naturally because of your position at address.

Never try to scoop the ball up cleanly as this will result in a bladed shot that fires off at great speed.

2. Playing from under low branches

The address position will be the same as for the bare lie, however choice of club is critical. It will almost never be more than a 7 iron as usually you are just trying to play back onto the fairway.

Your back swing will probably be short and limited by the branches. To keep the ball flight low, your finish must be very short.

Caution. *Avoid using a long club such as a 3 or 4 iron in an attempt to keep the ball flight low. This often results in a poor impact with the ball and sends it scuttling along the ground and staying in trouble!*

---

3. Buried ball in a bunker

This shot is not as difficult as it first appears. Basically you take your normal bunker stance, close the clubface so that it digs deeper into the sand and then play your normal bunker shot except that you must be ready for the impact; your wrists must be firm and you must accelerate through impact.

Because the ball is buried the resistance with the sand upon impact is greater than in a normal bunker shot and the clubface will be forced open. This usually provokes a slightly lower ball flight with more roll upon contacting the green.

Chapter 10.
Managing golf's two
ultimate adversaries

Jack Nicklaus with John Norsworthy

"Success depends almost entirely on how effectively you learn to manage the game's two ultimate adversaries: the course and yourself." ~ Jack Nicklaus

"The average golfer's problem is not so much a lack of ability as it is a lack of knowing what must be done." ~ Ben Hogan

Good course management is simply about assessing the situation in hand and making the best choice for your next shot. My advice is to keep things simple and follow these 5 golden rules:

1. Tee up to take trouble out of play

To play to the left side of the fairway, tee up on the right. To play to the right, tee up on the left.

When playing from a tee with trouble to one side, such as a water hazard, out of bounds or a sand trap, we instinctively tee up on the opposite side in an attempt to get away from the trouble. Well, this is the one time you must do the opposite of what your instinct tells you.

For example, on your tee shot there is an out of bounds to the right of the fairway and ideally you want to play to the left side of the fairway. In this case you should tee up on the right-hand side of the teeing area to open up the left side of the fairway and to take the trouble on the right out of play.

You can also apply this advice if you have a tendency to slice or hook. For a slice tee up on the right side to open up the left side of the fairway leaving more room for your shot to come back on the fairway, if you hook tee up on the left side.

2. Play your personal par

Golf is a rewarding experience no matter at what level you play and one of the best management techniques for a handicap player, although very simple, can dramatically improve your attitude and your score. It is to play your own par rather than the course par.

For example, the personal par for a 24-handicapper is an average of 12 bogeys and 6 double bogeys. For the 24-handicap player this is par golf – remember this!

To help you play your personal par, the best on-course aid is to create your own personal par scorecard. For the 24-handicapper, do this by adding two shots on each the six toughest holes on your course scorecard (shown as stroke indexes 1 to 6 on the score card) and one shot for the rest of the holes (stroke indexes 7 to 18).

Hole	1	2	3	4	5	6	7	8	9	Total
Par	4	5	3	4	4	4	3	4	5	36
Stoke Index	11	3	13	15	1	7	17	9	5	
Hole	10	11	12	13	14	15	16	17	18	
Par	3	5	4	3	4	4	4	3	5	35
Stoke Index	18	8	4	14	2	12	6	16	10	

Typical score card showing par for the course

Hole	1	2	3	4	5	6	7	8	9	Total
MyPar	5	7	4	5	6	5	4	5	7	48
Stoke Index	11	3	13	15	1	7	17	9	5	
Hole	10	11	12	13	14	15	16	17	18	
MyPar	4	6	6	4	6	5	6	4	6	47
Stoke Index	18	8	4	14	2	12	6	16	10	

Modified score card showing your personal par

From now on when looking at your scorecard, the pressure of trying to play the course par will disappear.

For example, if you start with a score of 5, 7, 4 you no longer need to panic and think "Help, I'm already 4 over after 3 holes". Instead you will feel calm in the knowledge that you are in fact level par for your handicap.

Also, do not expect to make all the greens in regulation. By adjusting the course par to your personal par, you change your strategy and your attitude when playing each hole. For example, rather than trying to reach the green on a par four in two shots, and in doing so forcing errors, play your personal par instead. This could mean that you have three, or perhaps even four, shots to reach the green. You may then find that you land your approach shot close enough to the hole to make a one putt to hole out.

This simple course management strategy will improve your attitude immensely allowing you to play more freely and with confidence.

3. Stay in the right frame of mind

I mentioned earlier Arnold Palmer's reply to the journalist when he was asked, "what is the most important shot in golf?" His reply was, "the next one".

The power of this seemingly casual comment cannot be overstated. Use it as part of your overall philosophy that you take with you to the golf course each time you play. It will help you develop a whole new attitude and to play just one shot at a time, which is essential for playing good golf and lowering your handicap.

Golf does of course take a lot of willpower and concentration but only for a very short time span, which is during the preparation and playing of each shot. The rest of the time you can relax and enjoy the beauty of what you see around you.

As once said by another very famous player Walter Hagen

"Don't hurry, don't worry, take time to smell the flowers!"

This is great advice when playing golf and for life in general. And remember, walk with your head held high – don't look down at the ground – the rough and other obstacles are only in your mind.

4. Choose the best club for the shot

I often see high handicap players choose a club that is inappropriate for the job in hand. Here are a few simple guidelines that will noticeably improve your scores.

Get the ball safely into play

Frequently in an attempt to gain distance off the tee, amateur players often choose a driver with insufficient loft (less than 10 ½ degrees) and often use their driver to get the ball into play even when a wood may be more suitable.

In most cases precision and not distance is the main priority when teeing off. To increase your accuracy from the teeing area, use a driver with more loft (11 degrees or more) and/or use a higher lofted club such as a 3 or a 5 wood. Doing so will produce more consistent results.

In the rough, take your medicine. Just play out of the rough using a club that is sure to get you back into play on the fairway such as a 9 iron or an 8 iron. While you may be tempted to play a longer club to gain a few extra yards, you are in fact taking a big risk. Longer clubs have a lower loft and usually get caught up in the long grass and you are likely to move the ball forward by only a few yards. Worse, you may land the ball once again in the rough.

Attack the greens long

Many amateurs come up short of the green when attacking the flag. Next time when on the course, try playing to the back of the green each time. This more aggressive attitude will produce much better shots and will also give a margin of error for the shot not so well struck.

Choose a club that you know is sufficiently long to get the ball to the target without forcing. By not playing every shot at the limit, you will play better and more consistently.

Around the greens, be wily like a Scot

Choosing the safest and most effective club for shots around the greens can save you several strokes per round, while choosing the wrong club can *cost* you several strokes. Follow these simple rules and you will be surprised what a big difference they make to your overall score.

The golden rule here is to use the putter wherever possible. A bad putt will usually end up closer to the hole than a bad chip or a bad pitch. When putting, just remember 'read it (the line), roll it, hole it'.

Learn also to use the putter from off the green. The 'Texas wedge' is a technique that helps where you can not get the putter face cleanly to the back of the ball because, for example, the ball is sitting down in longer grass. Using the putter, strike slightly down on the ball, it will pop up and out and then roll.

If putting is not an option, then be more like the wily Scottish golfers and chip and run the ball rather than trying to pitch it. Chipping leaves the ball closer to the hole more often than pitching which means fewer putts and of course fewer shots per round!

Chip using a 6 or 7 iron from 20 yards and in. The ball should fly just enough to get out of the fringe and start rolling on the green as soon as possible. A 5 wood (or hybrid) is very effective for chipping when the ball has nestled down into the fringe. The blades of grass move around the clubface, making the club less likely to snag and reduces the chances of grass getting between the ball and the clubface which causes great inconsistency of shots.

When you do use the sand wedge to pitch your approach to the green, make sure you use it only from good lies. If the ground is very hard the bounce on the sole of the club will favor 'thin' shots (striking the ball with the leading edge of the club) and if very soft it will favor 'fat' shots (striking the ground before hitting the ball).

5. What you bring is what you swing

There is an old saying "If you have not taken your swing to the first tee, you won't find it there". It means that once you start playing, practice time is over and if you haven't got your swing at the first tee, you won't find it by endlessly swinging the club.

Instead forget about swing mechanics, forget about 'how' and just remember to "*find the ball with the club head*".

Emergency breakdown service

More often that we would like to admit there are times during a round when the "wheel comes off " meaning that nothing is going well and your confidence sinks to its lowest ebb.

In these cases, and as suggested in a very well known book *The Hitchhikers Guide to the Galaxy,* the very first thing to do is: DON'T PANIC!

Instead, in a calm state of mind do as follows:

1. Choose a club for the next shot and make a few half-swings using your right hand only. Do this a few times until the movement produces a sensation of fluidity and easiness. Your arm should feel completely free from the shoulder down.

2. Now with both hands do the same thing and continue to allow the free-swinging sensation. No tightness or stiffness should be felt here and that disconnected feeling that the arms are swinging freely should continue.

3. Now step up to the ball, keep your eye on it and swing with that very soft and smooth feeling. The improvement in your ball striking will be immediate and your confidence will quickly start to return.

This is a simple exercise to get you back to the clubhouse in reasonable shape. A more thorough training session may be needed if this happens frequently.

Comment: *Next time you watch a tournament on the television, just check on how many pros go through this simple pre-swing routine to keep free of tension!*

Morgan Mason and John Norsworthy

Chapter 11. Questions and answers

Q. What is the most effective way to practice?

A. To internalize the correct movements so that they become instinctive, the exercises in this book must be repeated regularly.

At least one third of all your practice time should be devoted to forming the correct reflexes rather than solely striking balls.

When playing on the course you can *not* work on your swing so you must get the work done beforehand. And always remember the saying:

> *"If you have not taken your swing to the first tee, it's not there that you will find it".*

To get the most from your practice sessions, keep in mind the following points:

- Always do some stretching before the session.

- Start with small shots from a low tee before moving up to a longer club and longer shots.

- Hit 10 balls with your feet together.

- For the more advanced player, practice the 3-shape drill: try to hit 5 slices, 5 hooks then 5 straight shots.

Take time between each ball to observe the result and feel the sensation achieved. Remember it is quality not quantity that counts.

- If at any time you feel that you have lost your swing, go back to the exercises in "Chapter 4. Develop your natural ball-striking skills" on page 23. You will find your swing again very quickly, the exercises never fail.

- Always finish a training session with some putting. Do not go from the practice range directly to your car – every visit to the range must include at least 15 minutes of putting.

- To warm up before playing on the course, hit 2 or 3 balls with each club starting with the short irons and finishing with tee shots.

Q. Why am I so inconsistent?

A. There are many reasons for inconsistent play, but here are the most common:

- If your head is full of technical instructions and tips, you will freeze up and your playing will become unnatural, you will experience 'paralysis by analysis'. Follow the advice in this book and keep things as simple as possible and just concentrate on *finding the ball with the club head.*

- Often amateurs take far too many risks by trying to play shots that even a pro would not attempt. Always play the easiest and safest shot that you are certain that you can play.

- Bad club choice is a major cause of inconsistency. For example, on a poor to medium lie with a long second shot to play, many novice players attempt to use a 3 wood. A safer and surer choice on this type of lie would be a 5 or 7 wood or a rescue/hybrid club – all are much easier to play and good results are almost guaranteed.

- Attempting to play the course par is for the scratch golfer (a player with a handicap of zero). Any time you forget this you will put yourself under undue pressure and make far more mistakes than you need to. Remember always to play your personal par rather than the course par (see page 78).

- If you try to hole all long putts rather than just lagging up to the hole, the pressure may cause you to finish too far from the hole with a resulting three putt rather than a two putt.

Q. How can I cure my slice?

A. A slice is caused by the clubface arriving open at impact and imparting sidespin to the ball. There are several reasons for this, the most common of which is the club head swinging on an out to in path.

To overcome this, firstly check that your grip is correct: it may need to be a little stronger (hands turned more clockwise on the grip) with the club held more in the fingers. This will help to promote a natural squaring of the club at impact.

If you continue to slice after correcting your grip, use your right hand to pass over the left through impact as if imparting topspin in a forehand tennis shot.

If you find your shots are now pulling directly left or hooking left, this is quite normal – the swing path of the club head is still coming from outside the target line to inside it. To correct the swing path, see "Swing on plane" on page 48.

Work on this exercise for just one week and you are likely to cure your slicing for good.

Q. Why do my woods and irons rarely work well at the same time?

A. This is mainly a question of rhythm. The human being is very cyclic and for this reason is not able to react the same way each day. Technically the golf swing is the same for all long shots, however the woods do need a more flowing action due to their length and the irons, being shorter, require a sharper and more compact movement.

So do not worry, it is rare to have these two always working together in sync on the same day but when they are, and if your putting is also on song, it's the moment when your handicap comes tumbling down.

Q. How can I putt better?

A. There is a really simple answer to this very important question and I would like you to take me seriously and think about the reply for a few minutes.

So often bad putting is the result of approach shots ending up too far from the hole and three putts become almost a certainty.

The next time you are on the course, give a little extra attention to your chipping and pitching and really concentrate on getting close to the hole. You will be very surprised to find that there will be almost no tension on the putting if the distance to the hole is much less.

For the high handicap player, two putts per hole is easily attainable.

Q. When should I upgrade to better equipment?

A. Whatever the cost of clubs that you buy, be sure that a professional checks that the lie, weight and shaft flex are correct for you. This advice is free at any good golf pro shop.

Often after two years of golf, players feel ready to move up to higher performance equipment. Be aware however that you still have to swing the club correctly and to find the ball with the club head. More expensive equipment will not do the job for you!

Q. At what age should a child start to learn?

A. My daughter Gabriella started putting at the age of 18 months; this is perhaps a little young but why not?

I believe it is never too early to start playing golf providing the parents do not push the children against their will. In our very popular junior program, we officially start lessons from the age of six, but even at this age their concentration span is very limited.

The average age of champions in almost every sport nowadays is much younger than a few decades ago, so we must assume that the age to start in any given sport is more precocious.

Q. I always hit the ground just before the ball, why?

A. Ninety percent of the time this very common fault is due to 'lazy legs'. There is a lack of weight transfer from the right to the left side before and during impact. As a result your weight remains mostly on your right foot causing your centre of gravity to be some distance before the ball – hitting the ground becomes inevitable.

As a quick fix, practice some half shots with the right heel off the ground during the entire shot to recreate the feeling of a correct transfer at impact. Then make the same swing with both feet on the ground but allowing your right heel to lift just before impact.

Rapidly, you will notice a great improvement.

There are other reasons, of course, for this fault and if still in difficulty in spite of this exercise, pop along to your local pro and he or she will soon show you how to correct the fault.

Q. Why do pro's make golf look so easy?

A. When asked, "How do you make golf look so easy?" Gary Player once said

"The more I practice, the easier it gets"

This is the real reason professionals make playing golf look so easy. A professional will be playing and practicing at least eight hours a day in order for his swing to become a reflex when on the course rather than a commanded action.

Amateurs rarely have the time or desire to do this much 'work' and in any case their goals are usually very different. Nonetheless, the more you practice with the counsel of a professional, the higher the likelihood of achieving a grooved swing.

Remember, it is always imperative to correctly finish your swing if you wish to swing easily and with power. See "Start with the finish" on page 41.

Q. How often should I practice?

A. In reply to the same question, here are two famous quotes:

"Too much is not enough" ~ Gary Player

"Don't play too much golf. Two rounds a day are plenty." ~ Harry Vardon

Because so little time is spent hitting a ball on the course, it is absolutely necessary to practice if you want to improve.

Let me give you an example of the time spent actually striking balls when playing a round of golf for an average player who shoots 100.

A golf shot takes approximately 1.5 seconds, but I will be generous and round this up to 3 seconds per shot. This gives a total of 300 seconds or 5 minutes per round. Of those 5 minutes, forty percent of the shots are putts, which leaves around 3 minutes of real practice every time you play 18 holes!

You may then ask, "If this is so, why am I so tired after a round?" Perhaps it is the walking or more likely the concentration, but it is surely not the 3 minutes you used on physically swinging the club.

Now you have the answer the question "is 3 minutes per round enough to improve my golf?". Likely it is not and this is why it has to be complemented with work on the practice area.

Q. Why does golf seem to so hard to learn?

There are several reasons that prevent an aspiring golfer from progressing. Some are due to the recent trend for a more 'technical' style of golf instruction while others come from the nature of the game:

A. 1. The ball doesn't move. In most racket and ball games, such as tennis and squash, we react to a moving ball coming towards us by getting into position and then making the shot. There is little time to analyze what is happening and how we will play the ball. The response is very much a 'sporting' or 'athletic' one.

In golf, however, the situation is quite different. The ball doesn't move and we do not merely react to it. Instead the ball just sits there waiting to be hit by a hefty golf swing, which gives us a lot of time to think, to analyze and ultimately to freeze. This phenomenon is popularly known as 'paralysis by analysis' which inevitably results in a swing nothing like the one you intended to make.

Surprisingly when we remove the ball from the equation, things get easier. Just think back to the number of times you have made beautiful practice swings when there is no ball to hit.

The reason is simple; when there is no ball there is no tension and no stress. There is far less to think about, to worry about and to analyze. To eliminate the tension you must focus only on the few essential swing basics shown in this book. In a very short time, your actual swing will become as good as those perfect practice swings.

A. 2. The golf swing happens quicker than thinking. The golf swing happens incredibly quickly. It takes less than two seconds from start to finish (the average swing time is 1.4 seconds).

In this extremely short time many striving golfers are thinking about five or six different things to do. Literally there is not enough time for your brain to process the information and send it to your body. Even the most talented professional could not do this without destroying all sense of rhythm and tempo.

Once again, by concentrating only on the few essential basics (shown in this book), your mind will be clear and at rest while remaining poised for action.

Q. How long will it take me to learn golf?

A. In fact we never stop learning to play this great game, so a simple answer is difficult. However my standard reply is something like this.

If you follow my advice and philosophy in this book it will be possible to be playing on a golf course within six months with a level of play that will give you pleasure and confidence in front of other players.

If you are a *complete beginner*, it will be necessary to start with a minimum of ten lessons over a four to six week period followed by one lesson a week or every two weeks for another six lessons.

Eventually after the initial phase of learning, one lesson every month is probably the best way to keep in form over the year and a guarantee not to fall into too many bad habits. Naturally, practice both on the range and on the course is indispensable.

Mark Mansfield   Morgan Mason   John Norswort

Afterword

If you were able to read this book when you had a quiet moment or two, then hopefully that time was sufficient to pass on my message to you.

The idea in this book, as with all of my teaching, is to expose you to the fundamental basics that enable novice and established golfers to play better golf in an easier way.

Some technically oriented instructional books can be very interesting and make for excellent reading. The problem however is that when the conscious part of the mind starts to try to relay instructions on how to move various parts of the body, the more instinctual part of the mind, the part we use to move naturally, takes a back seat.

The goal of this book, the sum of my teaching career, is to provide an approach backed by specific exercises that allow you to move in a harmonious way while bringing the club head into contact with the ball in the right manner, at the right moment and with useful speed.

We have seen that the golfers of over 100 years ago played in perhaps a far more liberated manner than his or her counterpart of today. They did not seem overly concerned about biomechanics in order to achieve a decent score and today's 'paralysis through analysis' did not exist. Instead the most important element to them was to have a swing with rhythm and timing, to look well at the ball and to develop excellent coordination.

I would just like to take off my hat to all the excellent professionals and amateurs that have written many books on golf in the past, believe me it is not easy. I hope that I have been able to, in my simple fashion, unravel some of the knots and that your future games will have a little less stress and far more positive results.

About the Author

John Norsworthy

John Norsworthy, son to Ernest and Elizabeth, was born in Guildford, England in 1937.

Living just a few minutes from the local golf course, John at the age of six started making regular visits there and under the guidance of a friendly member, a WWI veteran, he became acquainted with chipping, putting and the general rules of the game.

At the age of twelve, John started caddying and at seventeen he started a five-year apprenticeship as an assistant at the Roehampton, Wansted and Dulwich golf clubs just a few miles from the center of London.

In 1960 John played in The Open Championship at St. Andrews, which that year celebrated its centenary anniversary.

He found he had a natural calling as a teacher and in 1961, after qualifying as a British PGA pro, became the assistant pro at the Dulwich and Sydenham Hill Golf Club in London, England. During this time, he was a member of the British assistants team in a match against the Carris Trophy team (amateurs).

A couple of years later John became the head pro at the Radyr Golf Club in Wales. While there he also became captain of the South Wales PGA and a golf correspondent for the national TV channel TWW.

Following that, John worked for the British PGA to promote golf in Nigeria in Africa, where he also the founded the Nigerian PGA.

In the early 70s, golf was starting to bloom in the French Cote D'Azur and he was asked to become the head pro at the Valbonne-Opio golf club. He also spent a couple of years in Belgium as the head pro at the Royal Waterloo golf club, the same club where Henry Cotton had held the same position some years before. While there he frequently gave lessons to the King Léopold and became the cofounder of the Belgian PGA.

Finally he returned to the Cote D'Azur once again as the Valbonne head pro, then head pro at the Riveria Golf-Mandelieu Club in Cannes before becoming the director of the St. Philippe Golf Academy from its opening in 2002 until 2008.

Today John lives in the South of France with his wife Ida where he continues to share the magic of his **Good Golf is Easy** training program with his students.

Made in the USA
Lexington, KY
17 April 2012